D1031831

WITHDRAWN
PUBLIC LIBRARY
BROOKLINE

STEM CAREERS

CHEMIST

by R.J. Bailey

pogo

3 1712 01557 0917

Ideas for Parents and Teachers

Pogo Books let children practice reading informational text while introducing them to nonfiction features such as headings, labels, sidebars, maps, and diagrams, as well as a table of contents, glossary, and index.

Carefully leveled text with a strong photo match offers early fluent readers the support they need to succeed.

Before Reading

• "Walk" through the book and point out the various nonfiction features. Ask the student what purpose each feature serves.

• Look at the glossary together. Read and discuss the words.

Read the Book

• Have the child read the book independently.

• Invite him or her to list questions that arise from reading.

After Reading

• Discuss the child's questions. Talk about how he or she might find answers to those questions.

• Prompt the child to think more. Ask: Do you know anyone who works as a chemist? What projects has he or she been involved in? Do you have any interest in this kind of work?

Pogo Books are published by Jump!
5357 Penn Avenue South
Minneapolis, MN 55419
www.jumplibrary.com

Copyright © 2018 Jump!
International copyright reserved in all countries. No part of this book may be reproduced in any form without written permission from the publisher.

Library of Congress Cataloging-in-Publication Data

Names: Bailey, R.J., author.
Title: Chemist / by R.J. Bailey.
Description: Minneapolis MN: Jump!, Inc., [2017]
Series: STEM careers | Audience: Ages 7–10.
Includes bibliographical references and index.
Identifiers: LCCN 2017008860 (print)
LCCN 2017009936 (ebook)
ISBN 9781620317143 (hardcover: alk. paper)
ISBN 9781624965913 (ebook)
Subjects: LCSH: Chemistry–Vocational guidance–Juvenile literature. | Chemists–Juvenile literature.
CYAC: Vocational guidance.
Classification: LCC QD39.5 .B235 2017 (print)
LCC QD39.5 (ebook) | DDC 540.23–dc23
LC record available at https://lccn.loc.gov/2017008860

Editor: Jenny Fretland VanVoorst
Book Designer: Michelle Sonnek
Photo Researcher: Michelle Sonnek

Photo Credits: Adobe Stock: RTImages, 8. Alamy: Erik Isakson, 10–11. Getty: Don Farrall, 9; Troy House, 14–15; Fuse, 16–17; Digital Vision, 18. iStock: GregorBister, 5. Shutterstock: Africa Studio, cover, 6–7, 20–21; Rachel Brunette, 1; Dmitry Melnikov, 3; Patrick Foto, 4; wavebreakmedia, 12–13; Nachaphon, 23; Andrezej Wilusz, 23. Thinkstock: Brand X Pictures, 19.

Printed in the United States of America at Corporate Graphics in North Mankato, Minnesota.

TABLE OF CONTENTS

CHAPTER 1

CHEMICALS EVERYWHERE!

Chemicals are everywhere. They are the building blocks of all matter. They make up the food you eat. They make up the water you drink. They make up the air you breathe. You are wearing them now!

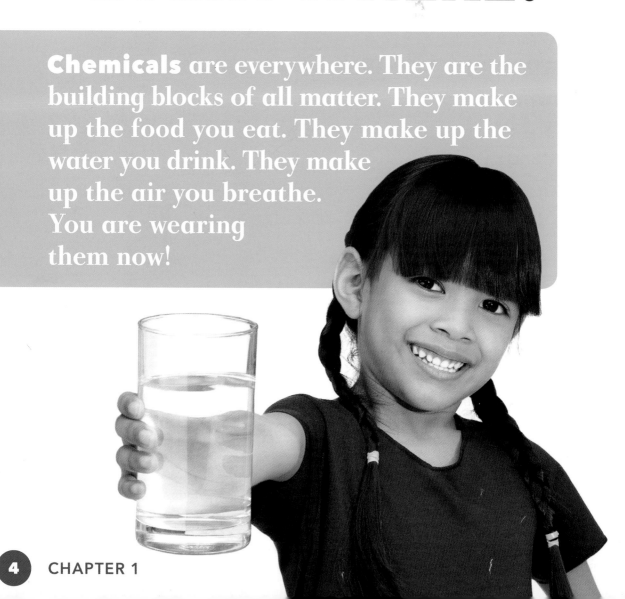

Chemists study matter and the chemicals that make it. Their work makes us safer. For example, they might study water to see how much lead is in it. Lead is not safe.

They invent new useful things. They might create a new pain reliever. They might invent a stronger, harder kind of plastic.

They make the things we use better. They might create a new **additive** for gas so that it burns cleaner.

DID YOU KNOW?

Chemistry is the study of matter. Because everything is made of matter, chemistry is at the heart of all the sciences. That is why it is known as the central science.

CHAPTER 2

WHAT DO THEY DO?

All matter is made up of chemicals. At their most basic level, chemicals are atoms, molecules, and **compounds**. An atom is the smallest unit of matter. Molecules are groups of atoms that bond together.

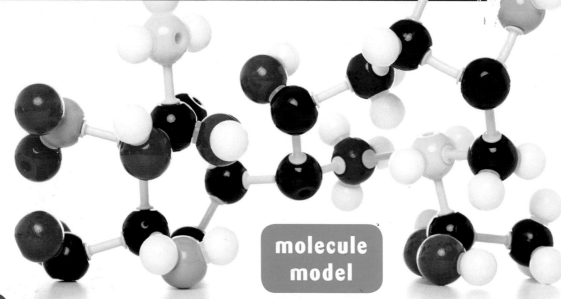

molecule model

Chemists study the atoms and molecules in **substances**. They mix substances. They study what happens. They describe what they see, smell, or feel. They look for a **reaction**.

Chemists usually work in labs. There they have access to a wide variety of tools. They use **beakers** to mix substances. They use **flasks** to store them. They use scales to weigh them. They use burners and lasers to heat them.

They use microscopes to study the chemicals' structures. They use computers to study their results. They write reports. They share what they learn.

TAKE A LOOK!

The **periodic table** is a list of all the known elements. Elements are the simplest kind of substance. They cannot be broken down. The table groups elements based on shared qualities.

H	■ = Metals		■ = **Metalloids**				■ = Nonmetals										He
Li	Be											B	C	N	O	F	Ne
Na	Mg											Al	Si	P	S	Cl	Ar
K	Ca	Sc	Ti	V	Cr	Mn	Fe	Co	Ni	Cu	Zn	Ga	Ge	As	Se	Br	Kr
Rb	Sr	Y	Zr	Nb	Mo	Tc	Ru	Rh	Pd	Ag	Cd	In	Sn	Sb	Te	I	Xe
Cs	Ba	La	Hf	Ta	W	Re	Os	Ir	Pt	Au	Hg	Tl	Pb	Bi	Po	At	Rn
Fr	Ra	Ac	Rf	Db	Sg	Bh	Hs	Mt	Ds	Rg	Cn	Nh	Fl	Mc	Lv	Ts	Og

Ce	Pr	Nd	Pm	Sm	Eu	Gd	Tb	Dy	Ho	Er	Tm	Yb	Lu
Th	Pa	U	Np	Pu	Am	Cm	Bk	Cf	Es	Fm	Md	No	Lr

Aromatic hydrocarbons contain conjugated double bonds. The most important example is benze— —struct— —which —s formu— —kule— —t— —d the —ar— —ple for explain— —re E— —tion— Cycle com— —fer— by the— —iz— elect—

Chemists can work alone or in teams. They may work with other scientists, such as **biologists** or **geologists**. They may work with **engineers**.

Many chemists work for private companies. They work for drug companies. They work in factories. Others work in government labs. They teach at universities.

CHAPTER 3

BECOMING A CHEMIST

Do you like learning how things work? Do you like to do experiments? A career as a chemist may be a good fit for you.

Science Fair

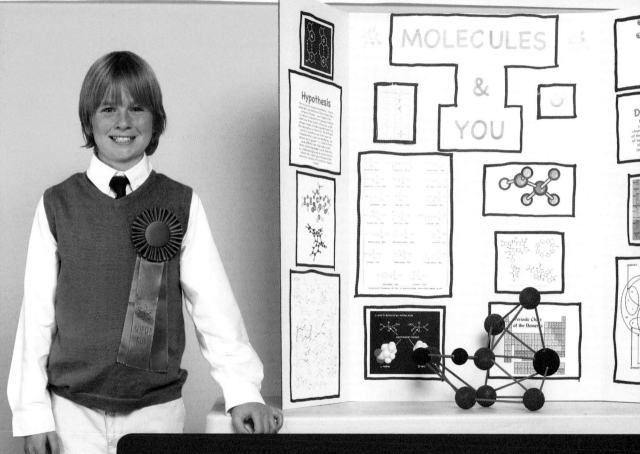

In school, take chemistry classes. Study math. Join your school's science club. Do a science fair project. Do experiments in your free time.

Later you will need a college degree.

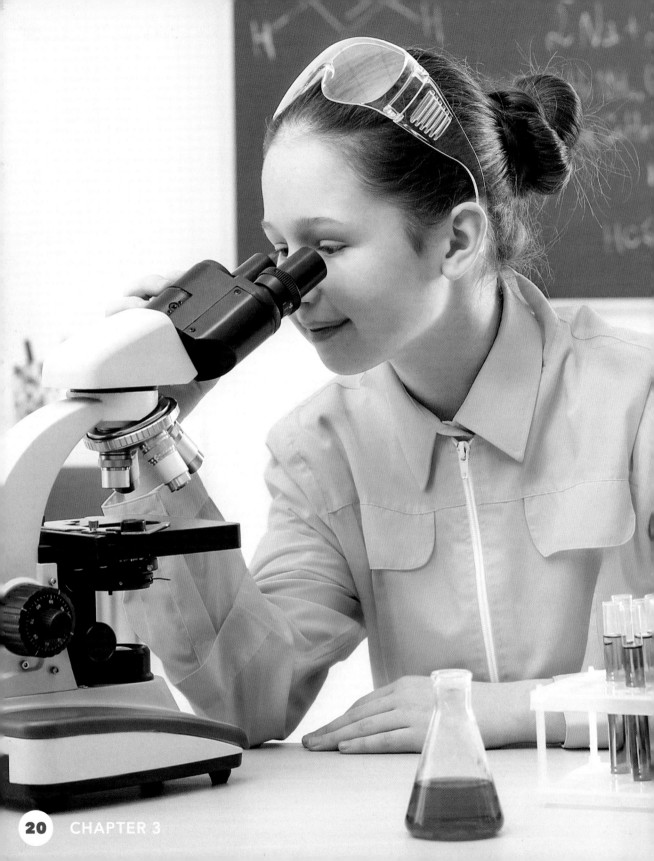

As a chemist, you can shape the future. How? You could find new forms of energy. You could make a new drug that helps the sick. You could find new ways to make foods grow better. The discoveries you can make are endless!

DID YOU KNOW?

To work as a chemist, you need STEM skills. What does STEM stand for? Science. Technology. Engineering. Math. STEM careers are in demand. They pay well, too.

ACTIVITIES & TOOLS

BATH FIZZERS

Want to practice chemistry and give someone a gift for the tub? Make bath fizzers!

What You Need:

- 1 cup baking soda
- ½ cup Epsom salt
- ½ cup citric acid (craft store)
- bath coloring tablets (optional)
- baking molds or plastic eggs
- 1 Tbsp. water
- 3 Tbsp. olive oil
- mixing bowl
- cup

1. In the bowl, mix the baking soda, Epsom salt, and citric acid.
2. If you are adding colors, crush several bath coloring tablets and add them into the bowl.
3. In the cup, mix the water and olive oil.
4. Quickly pour the liquid into the bowl. Mix everything together.
5. It will start to fizz. That's the chemical reaction! Stir until it's well mixed.
6. Scoop some of the mixture into one of your molds. You can use a muffin tin, baking molds, or plastic eggs.
7. Press the mix into the molds. Pack it tightly. If it seems too dry, mix in a few drops of olive oil.
8. Let your fizzers dry for about six hours. Take them out carefully.
9. Wrap them as gifts, or use them in your own bath. Drop them in the water and watch them fizz and melt!

additive: A substance added to another in small amounts to give or improve desirable qualities or decrease unwanted qualities.

beakers: Deep glasses with lips for pouring.

biologists: Scientists who study living organisms and life processes.

chemicals: Substances that cannot be broken down without changing into something else.

chemistry: A science that deals with the structure of substances and the changes that they go through.

chemists: Scientists who study the structure of substances.

compounds: A combination of two or more elements.

engineers: People who use math and science to solve society's problems and create things that humans use.

flasks: Glass bottles used in science experiments.

geologists: Scientists who study the history of Earth as recorded in rocks.

metalloids: Chemical elements that have properties common with both metals and nonmetals.

periodic table: An organized list of known elements; each is listed by its atomic number and mass.

reaction: A chemical change that happens when two or more substances combine to form a new substance.

substances: Physical materials with a specific chemical makeup.

INDEX

TO LEARN MORE

Learning more is as easy as 1, 2, 3.

1) **Go to www.factsurfer.com**

2) **Enter "chemist" into the search box.**

3) **Click the "Surf" button to see a list of websites.**

With factsurfer, finding more information is just a click away.

12|17

MAIN LIBRARY
BROOKLINE PUBLIC LIBRARY
361 Washington Street
Brookline, MA 02445